FOCUS ON
SCARF
Styling

LAYLA BARRON

PHOTOGRAPHS BY ASLAM LEVY

DEDICATION

I dedicate this book to my twin daughters,
Maryam and Gaseenah,
In the hope to inspire them and all Muslim sisters
to uphold the identity and values of Islam, Insha-Allah.

• ACKNOWLEDGEMENTS •

Writing this book has been a challenge and I would like to thank
the following people for making this book a reality .

1. My husband, Ridwaan and son, Ubaiduraghmaan for their motivation, patience and support throughout.

2. My mother, sisters, sisters-in-law, my friends and colleagues who inspired the initial enthusiasm and who so readily availed their scarves.

3. The models used in this book for their patience and endurance.

4. Mr. Shaik who spent many hours filming the portfolio.

5. Mr. Jedaar and Sheikh E. Gabriels for their motivation and advice.

6. Aslam Pieterse, Zainunesa Allie, Fatima Abdurahman and Surayda Adams for assisting me with the draping of some styles.

7. Mardia Hendricks, Sajida Gaffoor and Anwar Gydien who spent hours typing the manuscript.

8. Sheigh Adiel Davids for assisting me in the choice of Quranic verses and Ahadith.

9. A special thanks to the photographer, Aslam Levy, for his professional advice, kindness, patience and for sacrificing most of his free time depicting all the colourful photos in this book.

Copyright © L. Barron 1994
This edition published in 1998 by
Hidden Treasure Press, P.O. Box 591 Gatesville 7766 South Africa
Edited by Mogamat Toffar
Photographs by Aslam Levy
Cover Photo by Yunis Muhammed
Design and Layout by Abdullah Amien
DeskTopRepro by Mogamat Faiez Martin
Printed and bound by National Book Printers, Goodwood, Western Cape

ISBN 0-9584176-9-5

• CONTENTS •

PREFACE

*W*hile learned Muslim writers and scholars throughout the world involve themselves in discourses on the ideological polemics of Islam, argue on different fatwa and often condemning each other to fates worse than death, a sister living here and now, concerned with translating Islamic values into practical living, writes a book on scarf-styling. How refreshing to see someone consider this life worth living and living well – with the emphasis on the values of Islam.

Like the traditional cook book which considers the needs of the Muslim eater, this book focuses on a part of a woman's dress, her headgear, and makes a statement: headgear can be attractive – more attractive than hairstyles! This is a courageous challenge that Layla Barron presents to all her readers, Muslim and non Muslim women alike: just follow the instructions, step by step, and feel the need to cover the hair.

Interestingly, the numerous instructions and illustrations are interspersed with pearls of wisdom from Qur'an and Ahadith on which to reflect while practising the styles, which add another dimension to this book – Islamic propagation. Young Muslim women who feel the urge to succumb to the "exciting" and "attractive" fashions advertised on the tabloids of the TV and magazines, may seriously be searching for an alternative to the eurocentric styles which disregard the prescriptions of the Shari'ah and deprive them of their dignity. Layla asserts such values as decency, simplicity, purity and goodness in the selection of clothing and subtly draws out her readers, young and old alike, to try, and in the process become assertive and creative.

Focus on Scarf-styling is a tremendous step forward – the ethos, the presentation and the content – in the Muslim community's search for guidance in living the Shari'ah. It is hoped that more How-do-I books would appear covering every facet of life of a Muslim, and, thereby, empowering young people to proudly reassert their identity as Muslims in belief and practice – (if Allah wills).

MUHAMMAD RASHARD JEDAAR

Administrator: Islamic College of Southern Africa

23 August 1994

ICOSA

AUTHORS
PREFACE

*L*ike many working women in a western society, I find myself having to choose a mode of dress that is Islamically acceptable, beautiful, as well as comfortable.

Although I do not have any special training in scarf styling, I believe that my feministic yearning to look presentable, to clothe myself according to the principles of Islam, and trying to uphold my Islamic identity in a western society motivated me to experiment with various scarf styles. To satisfy this yearning, I found myself always on the lookout for new ideas and modifying the old.

It is stated in the holy Quraan, chapter 2 verse 185

" Allah intends every comfort for you. He does not want to put you to difficulties."

From the above verse it is apparent that it is the people who make religion difficult. Thus, we should not feel trapped by covering our heads. On the contrary it should be seen as a means of preserving our dignity and purity. Scarves should be seen as a means of enhancing ourselves, for it can make a significant change to our self-image. It can, depending on specific styles, enhance your looks, making you look younger, more mature or sophisticated. Most of all, it makes a huge difference to your self-confidence when you are striding out into the world.

In compiling styles for this book I tried to use as many different fabric and styles to enable you to make the most of the various types of scarves you possess.

It is my sincerest wish that Muslim women should use this book as a guide to dress themselves fashionably but in accordance to Islam.

LAYLA BARRON

INTRODUCTION

بَنِیۤ اٰدَمَ قَدۡ اَنۡزَلۡنَا عَلَیۡکُمۡ لِبَاسًا ٣٦
یُّوَارِیۡ سَوۡاٰتِکُمۡ وَرِیۡشًا
وَلِبَاسُ التَّقۡوٰی ذٰلِکَ خَیۡرٌ

"O ye children of Adam! We have bestowed
clothing upon you to cover your shame, as
well as to be an adornment to you. But the
clothing of righteousness,
that is best....."

Al-Quran: VII: 26

*I*n addition to protection against the elements, we clothe ourselves to cover our shame and as a means of beautifying ourselves. In the verse quoted above, Allah, in His Infinite mercy, permits us to cover our shame as well as adorning ourselves while reminding us of cultivating our inner beauty.

The dilemma facing our womenfolk today is simple: how can we dress beautifully without sacrificing our Islamic values? Do we need to ape the fashions of our sisters in the West and risk losing our identity as Muslims and our individuality as creative beings? Certainly not. Islam, as a way of life, prescribes values through the Shari'ah and gives Muslims the freedom to create high standards of living, which encompasses dressing, eating and, generally, living within the parameters of the Shari'ah. We can design and wear our clothes to cover our shame and feel confident when we stride into the world with our Islamic garb.

Islamic dress, of which the headgear forms an integral part, liberates women from the stranglehold of the fashion world, and more important, facilitates moving about freely and fulfilling their daily duties and 'ibadat (acts of worship). A disturbing trend, so prevalent among our sisters, is to discard the wearing of a scarf – which is often seen as the least attractive of their clothing, out of fear of being labelled out of fashion or simply out of ignorance of scarf-styling.

Scarf-styling has been developed primarily to focus attention on the significance of the headgear in a woman's appearance, to encourage and conscientise our sisters to wear the headgear and to introduce an exciting variety of scarf styles. In this book the author presents a variety of styles for different occasions and while they appear intricate, they are so easy to follow and style that one may wonder why one did not think of it before. It is also the purpose of this book to stimulate the reader's creative flair into adding to the growing repertoire of scarf styling.

• BASIC DRAPING TIPS •

Styling your scarf is quick and easy to do, with only a few basic rules to follow in order to complete all styles in this book successfully.

1. HOW TO USE THIS BOOK :

For your convenience this book is divided into various chapters. Where possible each style is introduced with a cover photo to give you an idea of how the style looks, the type of face it is well suited for and the type of scarves that can be used to style the specific scarf.

Step-by-step photos as well as clear instructions are given to assist you. It should however be kept in mind that this book only serves as a guide, for sizes and textures of scarves vary a great deal. Thus, if you do not use the basic size of scarves you will need to adjust your styling.

At the bottom of the step-by-step instructions, hints and variations of the specific style are given. Illustrations of some of these variations are also given, although it is not described fully. Here you follow the basic steps and adjust accordingly.

This book is mainly based on how to bring out specific designs in a scarf. So before choosing a style, determine which part of the scarf you want highlighted, eg. the borders, corners, specific flowers etc.

WHEN CHOOSING A SPECIFIC STYLE KEEP THE FOLLOWING IN MIND :

1)The type of function. Is the chosen style suitable for the occasion?
2) Does the colour and style suit you?
3) After pinning a style, see if the occasion allows you to further enhance your scarf using brooches etc.

2. THE IMPORTANCE OF AN UNDERSCARF.

Most of the styles in this book are pinned onto an underscarf. The scarf will only remain firm on your head if the underscarf or undercap is properly secured. Some non-slip scarves and a few styles in this book do not require underscarves. Whenever a scarf needs to be pushed forward, it is important to pull only the edges of the underscarf or undercap forward in order not to disturb the style of the top scarf.

3. HOW TO PIN:

The best pins to use are the long, thin steel pins. The thicker pins tend to leave holes in the fabric of the scarves and do not penetrate some fabrics easily. When pinning try not to leave pins too visible. Scarves are usually pinned at the beginning, ending or overlapping of specific drapes. Pins should be pinned through underscarf or undercap as well. Follow instructions to determine positioning of pins. I find the best way of pinning to be:

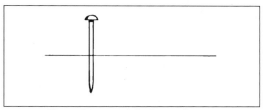

Keep pin up straight on overlap,etc.

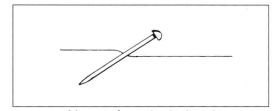

Move pin forward or backward.

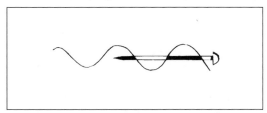

Slip pin underneath fabric, picking up fabric.

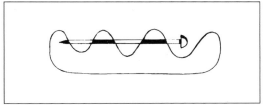

Move pin through fabric as if tacking it.

4 CORSAGE PINS:

Apart from being decorative, corsage or kilt pins give a firmer grip. I usually find that pinning one such pin on the last drape of my top scarf, or on the crown of my head, secures the scarf a little longer.

5. FABRIC USED

The styles in this book are divided into rectangular, square and triangular scarves.

Scarves can be made using any type of fabrics from soft flowing ones to stiff, crisp ones.

Silk, viscose, cotton, chiffon, wool, muslin, etc. are nowadays used to make scarves or bands.

6. SCARF SHAPES

6.1 Size of rectangular scarves.

Sizes of rectangular scarves vary a great deal, but for convenience sake we used the basic measurements of 1.58 metres by 0.58 metres. It should, however, be kept in mind that the longer the scarf the more can be done with it. For beginners I would suggest that they use the basic measured scarf.

Four starting points are used:

6.1.1 Firstly, starting from the narrower side of rectangle - remember to overlap the points at the nape of head if scarf is wide enough. It will keep your scarf firmer on your head.

6.1.2 Secondly, centre the longer side of scarf - at times it will be found that the second half will be too short to go around neck. If that is the case, try to bring point of scarf around and centre it on crown of head or at beginning, instead of centring the scarf, make one side longer than the other.

6.1.3 Thirdly: Start near the edge of scarf... especially when tying bands or scarves around head. This can also be done with Midoras in order to cover neckline.

6.1.4 Fourthly: Start at the back of head especially for turbans or for knot styling.

6.2 Triangular scarves

Sizes of triangular scarves vary a great deal. Isosceles triangular scarves with the baseline of approximately 1.5m (150cm) can easily be used for most of the styles in this book. It should be borne in mind that the effect of the styling will be influenced by the designs and edges of the particular scarf. Triangular scarves can also be used to form bands.

6.3 Square scarves

Square scarves can be used as is eg. Midoras or it can be folded diagonally to be used as a triangular scarf or a band. See triangular styling.

7. CHOICE OF STYLING

Scarves must not look like a separate entity to your outfit. It must blend in to form part of your outfit. Choose accessories carefully in order not to be over-dressed. When matching scarves and clothing keep in mind the different designs, colours and textures.

Experiment with styles and colouring which suits and enhance your personal taste. Remember, at first you may feel self-conscious wearing a specific scarf style but as people start complimenting you, the desire to experiment will supersede. As you become more agile in pinning, various styles can be combined to form a new style. Be versatile and use the basic ideas given in this book as a guideline to create your own styles.

8. ACCESSORIES

For special functions:

1)Enhance style further by positioning brooches and hair or hat bows on side, back or front view of scarf depending on chosen style (see back view of scarf.)

2)Bows can also be formed by using the excess part of scarf (see Two-Tone turbans)

3)Strings of pearls, cord, chains and alice bands can also be used to supplement roll bands or can be incorporated to form part of band.

4)Hats and berets can also be arranged to suit a particular occasion.

5) Earrings.

With some elaborate scarf styling, it is superfluous to use earrings. Scarves can thus be pinned close to the ear. One earring can be worn for styles with bows on side of head especially Petal Styling. For turban styling it is more effective wearing hanging earrings.

The underscarf is the most important part when draping scarves.
It forms the basis upon which all scarves can be pinned.
The three basic forms of underscarves that can be used are the cap,
the age-old migram and the two-legged underscarf.

• UNDERSCARF CAP •

These caps are as easily available as it is to make. Cotton knit or soft ange-laise fabric used and can either be finished off by lace edges or decorated with beads. The fabric chosen should be non-slip and pins should be able to penetrate it easily. These caps are made to fit the head like a glove and are either controlled and adjusted by two strips or elastic at the back. So all you need to do is to place and adjust it on your head.

Fancy caps of which the front is padded and decorated with either embroidery or beading are now easily obtainable. These fancy caps can be worn as is or it can be incorporated with another scarf to cover neck. (see rectangular scarves, variation with bands).

Ahmad and Muslim relates:

"God is beautiful and He loves beauty."

• UNDERSCARF MIHRAM •

The age- old underscarf commonly known as Mihram, is a rectangular cloth preferably of muslin fabric or any non-slip fabric. It should measure approximately 150cm long and 40cm wide. I prefer using this because it sits firmly on the head and pins can be pinned onto it more easily. The technique of swinging a mihram is simple.

• METHOD OF SWINGING •

Step.1: Centre mihram tucking away hair. Pull front edges on both sides of head, twist it and bring opposite sides to front.

Step 2 : Hold front edge of first side steady by using lips. Pull edges of second side tight and fold in the form of a band.

Step 3 : Bring folded side around head and tuck remaining part under the mihram, at the back of head.

Step 4 : Starting with the first side, fold and bring around head. Tuck remaining part underneath.

• REMEMBER •

1. By pulling front edges of scarf (before starting with step 2), you can adjust the firmness of it on your head. Adjust to your liking (not too tight).

2. If your scarf moves back after a while, then DO NOT pull scarf forward rather pull the edges of underscarf forward. Thus you would not disturb the style of the top scarf.

• UNDERSCARF CHIFFON •

*When buying chiffon or georgette for a scarf, buy
approximately 1.5 metres and make your own
under and top scarf by dividing fabric in half.
By doing this it will eliminate the problem of the
underscarf being visible when draping top scarf.
It will further deepen the colour of the top scarf
you are wearing especially brighter colour scarves.*

• HOW TO CUT AND SEW •

Use a rectangular piece of material approximately 1.5 metre long.

1. Cut two long legs by halving the rectangle three quarters of the way.

2. Hem the sides that are not self-edged.

3. Take longest narrow side, tack it and ruche together by pulling the end of the tacking thread. This will form the head.

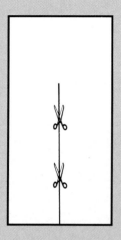
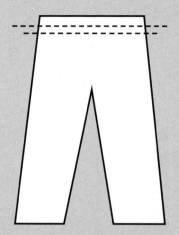

• IDEAS WITH THESE UNDERSCARVES •

• METHOD OF SWINGING •

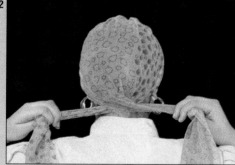

Step 1 : Centre ruched portion on head.

Step 2: Take sides to back of head and twist.

Step 3 : Fold sides and swing around head.

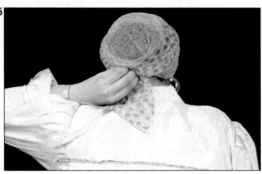

Step 4 : Let it overlap in the centre, proceed alternating sides until no more fabric left.

Step 5 : Tuck excess parts underneath.

• VARIATIONS •

1. When used as a turban. Choose fabric of outfit or matching chiffon.
2. For two tone turbans. Make two sides (legs) contrasting.
3. To cover neck. Follow step 1 and step 2. Keep enough fabric on one side to cover neck. Complete step 3 with shorter side. Step 4 - Cover neck with remaining side.

REMEMBER

Always try to use an underscarf that is more or less the colour of the top scarf.

• BASIC STYLE I •

Most of the styles in this book are created from either
of these two basic styles. It can also be worn as is
or can be incorporated with other styles.
This basic style gives you the advantage of having
ample scarf left to create various styles.
It also gives a lovely drape around the front
that will cover low-line dresses sufficiently.

• METHOD OF SWINGING •

Step 1: Centre at narrow side of rectangular scarf. Overlap edges of narrow side at back of head and pin.

Step 2: Take long side, with or without side border. Pin on side of head and bring remaining part around neck to other side and pin.

Step 3: Bring the excess around and pin on side of head and let remaining part hang loose over the shoulder.

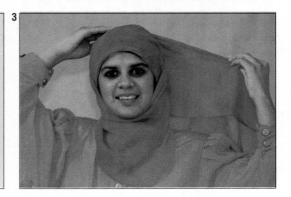

• VARIATIONS •

1. Two brooches connected with a chain or any other design can be worn on the side of head. (See back view of scarves.)

• HINTS •

1. If scarf cannot overlap at back (step.1.) pin at the furthest ends of scarf.

2. Decorative edges can either be draped around neck or shoulders (depending on Step 2) and the type of scarf used.

The Prophet (PBUH) said:

"Cleanse yourself, for Islam is cleanliness"

Ibn Hayyam

• BASIC STYLE 2 •

This basic style forms a beautiful flowing pattern at the back.
The part around the neck can be worn over dresses or
tucked away under neck-line to bring out bodice of dress.
This style brings out lines in scarves beautifully.
Various bands can also be incorporated with this style.

" A man should not look at the private parts of another man,
nor a woman of another woman ...."

Muslim

• METHOD OF SWINGING •

Step 1: Centre long side of rectangular scarf and pin on both sides of head.

Step 2: Pin first side of scarf on one side of head. Bring around to other side and pin. Take scarf further around and secure by pinning.

Step 3: Take point of second side of scarf (decorated edge). Pin in centre of head. Take sides and pin on both sides of head.

Or

Step 3 : Take narrow side of second side. Place around back of head. Pin on both sides of head.

• VARIATIONS •

Step 4 can be added where the back of the scarf are ruched together by pinning scarf at the back. (See back view of scarves.)

• PILLBOX • *(LONG BORDERS)*

ABU DAWOOD has related the tradition transmitted by AYESHA, the Prophet's wife, wherein she says:

Asma bint AbuBakr came to the Prophet
wearing thin clothes.
The Prophet turned his face away and said :
" When a woman reaches
puberty, it is not proper
that any portion of her body
should be seen by a man
except these parts,
(and he pointed to his
face and hands)"

10

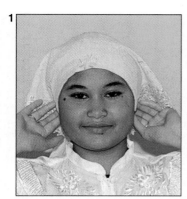

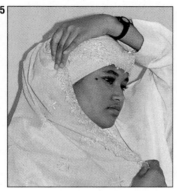

PILLBOX
(LONG BORDERS)

Use a rectangular scarf with borders or patterns (either embroidered, laced or beaded) on the longer side of rectangle. Various types of fabric can be used for this fold.

• METHOD OF SWINGING •

STEP 1 : Swing underscarf. Centre narrow side and pin ends or overlap, and pin at back of head.

STEP 2 : Bring sides up into bun. Fold bringing out pattern of scarf. Pin down.

STEP 3 : Bring fold around the front of head and pin on the other side.

STEP 4 : Open fold and pin both edges of fold.

STEP 5 : Using right side of fold, pin and bring around neck and bring to the other side.

STEP 6 : Take point of remaining part, pin the scarf centre and pin.

STEP 7 : Pin sides of scarf adjusting it around chin.

• VARIATIONS •

1. ELABORATE BORDER

1.1
STEP 1 : If border is too elaborate it can be folded away before starting.

1.2
If using a scarf with a beaded edge, do not pull step 3 too tight.

2. TO COVER FACE

STEP 5 : Bring over nose.

3. HOW TO ADJUST

After completing step 5. It sometimes happens that the one side is too short to go around head especially after you have folded border away. If this occurs do the following instead :
STEP 5 : Bring left side of fold around neck and pin on the other side.
Complete doing Steps 6 and 7 as above.

4. WAYS OF ENDING LAST SWING

4.1
STEP 6 : Centre point in front of forehead.
STEP 7 : As above.

4.2
STEP 6 : Centre point on crown of head.
STEP 7 : As above.

4.3
STEP 6 : Do not bring point to front. Take side further around crown of head and pin on side.
STEP 7 : Pin side and let it hang loose.

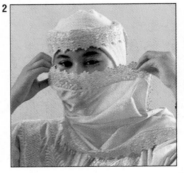

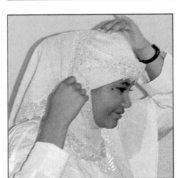

• TWISTING ROLL •

DUA (PRAYER) WHEN LOOKING IN A MIRROR

O Allah, as beautiful as you have created me,
beautify my character.

DUA (PRAYER) WHEN DONNING A GARMENT

"Praise be to Allah, who clad me with which I cover my shame
and with which I adorn myself in my life".

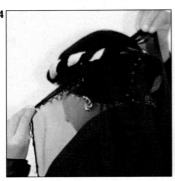

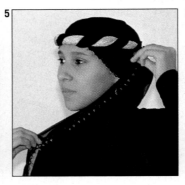

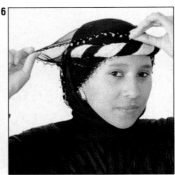

• TWISTING ROLL •

Use a rectangular scarf with or without borders . For variation use cords, string of pearls, bands, etc.

• METHOD OF SWINGING •

STEP 1: Put on underscarf. Start from narrow side. Pin scarf at back of head.

STEP 2: Bring sides up into bun. If using cord, etc., place it inside bun and secure by pinning.

STEP 3 : Twist band or cord evenly around the bulk of scarf. Place and pin completed roll on other side of head.

STEP 4 : Tuck away remaining band and open roll. Pin one of side roll on left side of head.

STEP 5 : Using right side of roll , pin on side of head and bring scarf around neck.

STEP 6 : Pin on other side and centre point as in previous style.

• VARIATIONS •

1. If using a full scarf as second colour.. Before starting STEP 1, turn a second colour around underscarf.

2. Bands can also be tucked under the underscarf, before starting STEP 2.

3. For perfect roll: When rolling band, keep remaining scarf steady and swing only border, band etc. around.

4. If scarf is too long: Before starting with top scarf in STEP 1. Fold narrow side. Then proceed styling.

5. This style can also be made using BASIC STYLE II depending on size of scarf.

6. This style can also be worn in the following ways:

6.1 Use a rectangular scarf with decorative edge

STEP 1 and 2 as above but do not insert cord, band or second scarf.

STEP 3 : Twist decorative edge evenly around bulk of scarf. Place and pin completed roll on other side of head.

STEPS 4, 5 and 6 follow through.

6.2 By forming a Halfmoon Roll in front.

STEP 1 and 2 as above but do not insert cord, band or second scarf.

STEP 3 : Twist decorative edge evenly around bulk of scarf. Pin just before the centre of forehead. Skip twisting, pin and twist further to the other side. (See photo.)

STEPS 4, 5 and 6 follow through.

1

6.3 Another way of forming a Halfmoon Roll in front:

STEP 1 : as above.

STEP 2 : Pin scarf on one side of head and bring it around to cover neck first. Pin on either side.

STEP 3 : Bring bulk of scarf round head, rolling as in STEP 3 of 6.2. Tuck remaining part away or let it hang on side. See p41 for variation.

2

3

• LAYERS •

The Prophet (P.B.U.H.) said:

Whoever says the following after wearing clothes,
all his sin will be forgiven:
"All praise is for Allah,
who clothed me with this dress,
which He bestowed upon me without efforts."

Bukhari / Abu Dawood / Tirmithi

*Use a rectangular scarf
with beaded edges or borders
on longer side of rectangle.
Fabric should not be too stiff.*

• METHOD OF **SWINGING** •

STEP 1 : Swing **underscarf**. Start from narrow side. Pin on both **sides** or at the back of head.

STEP 2 : Bring **border** around front. Pin on side.

STEP 3 : Space borders evenly and **pin** on other side. Repeat **until** just enough left to turn once more around head.

STEP 4 : Bring side up. Pin. Bring around to cover neck.

STEP 5 : Pin and **bring** over head while spacing.

STEP 6 : Pin on the other **side of head.**

• VARIATIONS •

FRONT VIEW

1. POINTED EFFECT

STEP 5 : Last turn. Pin point of scarf in centre front of head.

STEP 6 : Pin both sides of head.

STEP 5 : Last turn over head. Pin last side of scarf in centre front of head. Take both sides of centre pin. Take both sides of border further to the back and pin. (halfmoon).

STEP 6 : Pin both sides of head.

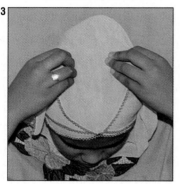

3. OVAL EFFECT

STEP 5 : Scarf as in round effect variation but take both sides of centre pin and pin edges even nearer to each other, getting an oval effect. Pleat the oval before pinning down.

BACK VIEW

RUCHED BACK

STEP 7 : Ruche top layer of scarf at back of head by pinning.

TO FURTHER ENHANCE THE RUCHED BACK.

1.1 A bow with contrasting colour matching the decorative edge can be pinned onto the ruching.

1.2 Brooches, artificial flowers etc. can also be used.

2. When centring the point use the decorative side instead.

• CENTRE PIECE •

Use a rectangular scarf with sides or corners that is decorative or MISFALS (a rectangular scarf with gold embroidered centre). This style emphasizes these centres and brings out the pattern or motive on scarf.

*"Most certainly (some of) you will follow the ways
of those before you inch by inch and yard by yard;
so much so that had one of them entered the narrow hole of a lizard,
you would also enter it; and so much so that had one of them had
sexual intercourse in the public (street), you would do the same."*

Bukhari / Muslim

• METHOD OF SWINGING •

SCARF WITH DECORATIVE
EDGE ON SHORTER SIDE OF
RECTANGLE.

Step 1: Swing underscarf.
Centre plain side of top scarf
and pin on both sides of head.

Step 2: Using one side. Choose
specific pattern. Bring over
head and around front and
centre it.

Step 3 : Bring edges around
head and secure by pinning.

Step 4 : Using second side, pin
and bring around neck.

Step 5 : Pin on other side and
bring further around head.

*Remaining part can hang over
shoulder.*

• VARIATIONS •

1.1. To enhance pattern even more:
Step 1 : Centre decorative edge instead.

1.2. To get border around neck :
Step 4 : Bring bordered edge to the other
side, pin and bring it around neck.

1.3. If preferred : Cover neck first doing step
4 and 5, Then bring pattern around (STEP 2
AND STEP 3)

1.4 Enhance back view further by placing
brooches, bows, etc.

• METHOD OF SWINGING •

(pattern in the centre of rectangular scarf)

Step 1: Instead of centring long side of scarf, centre narrow side.

Step 2: Centre pattern around forehead and pin both sides at the back of head.

Steps 3, 4 and **5** remains the same.

To enhance back see ideas for back view.

• PILLBOX II • *(SHORT BORDERS)*

*The Messenger of Allah
(PBUH) has clearly stated that
Allah condemns those men
and women who behave
and dress like one another*

(Bukhari)

Use a rectangular scarf with borders, patterns, scalloped edges or beading on the narrow side of scarf. This style is similar to the pillbox using longer borders but the effect is that it is more flatter around the head. This style is ideal to keep those slippery chiffon scarves firmer on your head.

• METHOD OF SWINGING •

Step 1 : Swing underscarf. Centre longer side of rectangular scarf and pin on both sides of head.

Step 2 : Use side with border (narrow side). Fold the width of the pattern or width preferred to bring out pattern.

Step 3 : Bring pattern over head. Centre it around forehead.

Step 4 : Overlap and pin two ends at back of head.

Step 5 : Using the second side of scarf. Pin it and bring around to other side of head.

Step 6 : Bring edge further around head and neck. Pin on other side of head. Let remaining part hang over shoulder.

• HINT •

1. Step 3: Take care not to pull pattern or border too tight around head.

2. Remember when folding , to keep decorative edge on top and pleat folds underneath it.

3. Step 5: If preferred, instead of bringing the bordered part around head, take the plain side around head.

4. If using a large rectangular scarf, fold to width measure approximately 50cm.

5. If folds occur on top, pull edges of Step 3 backwards to clear crown of head

• SINGLE AND DOUBLE POINTS •

The Holy Quran : 5:32

"And do not covet that by which Allah has made some of you excel others, men should have the benefit of what they earn and women shall have the benefit of what they earn."

This style I wish to attribute to the memory of a colleague and friend , the late Gadija Baba, the first person I saw wearing this style.

Use any rectangular scarf with decorative edges preferably a softer chiffon with beaded edge.

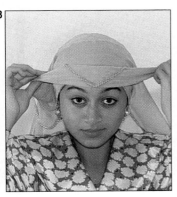

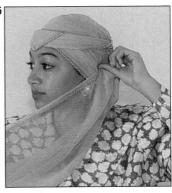

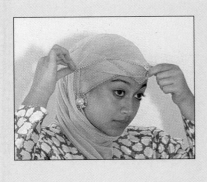

•METHOD OF SWINGING •

Step 1 : Swing underscarf. Centre longer side of scarf. Pin on both sides of head.

Step 2 : Use one side. Take hold of back point. The scarf should hang in the form of a triangle with point down.

Keep scarf in this position. Throw point of scarf repeatedly over backwards to form a roll or fold.

Step 3 : Bring around forehead. Centre it and pin underneath fold.

Step 4 : Bring end right around to back. Tie or pin ends together and tuck remaining parts away.

Step 5 : Pin second side on one side of head. Take point of second side. Centre and pin it.

• VARIATIONS •

1. Step 3: If a bordered edge is used. Start either from plainer side of rectangular scarf or start by centring the wrong side of the rectangular scarf. Otherwise your point in Step 3 will be on the wrong side.

2. For DOUBLE POINT Effect:
Step 6 : Place point just above first point.

3. Point can be turned Upwards:
Step 3 : Keep scarf in position. Throw point of scarf repeatedly to the front to form a roll.

4. Finish off with brooch.

• THE V •

Use a rectangular scarf with beaded or corded edges.
The longer the scarf the more V's can be formed.

" *And We have commanded man to be kind towards his parents. With*
trouble did his mother bear him, with trouble did she bring him forth; and
the bearing of him and the weaning of him was thirty months; until when
he attains his maturity and reaches forty years, he says: My Lord!
Arouse me that I may give thanks for your favour which you have
bestowed upon me and my parents, and that I may do good which pleas-
es you. And be gracious to me in the matter of my offspring. Surely I
turn to You and surely I am of those who submit (Muslims)"

Sura Al Ahqaf 46:15

• METHOD OF SWINGING •

Step 1: Swing underscarf. Centre long front edge of rectangular . Pin on both sides of head.

Step 2: Use side of scarf. Bring only edge to centre and pin it. Take remaining edge of scarf and bring back to side. Pin and tuck away.

Step 3: Pleat the inside of the V. Pull pleats tight and pin. (One V was thus formed.)

Step 4: Tuck remaining parts away under the bottom of the scarf.

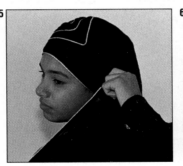

Step 5: Pin second side on side of head. Bring around neck and pin.

Step 6 : Bring further around either forming a V or keeping it straight. Pin.

• VARIATIONS •

A multitude of V'S can be made depending on the length of scarf.
Step 2 : Instead of tucking away, form smaller V's.

FOR BETTER EFFECT :

1. Let the V's stretch further than centre of head and space evenly.

2. V's can also be placed from the back making the points showing downwards or sideways.

• THE TWO TONE V •

V's with contrasting colours can be draped by using two rectangular scarves in contrasting colours.

There is a Tradition which says :
"Paradise lies at the feet of the mother."

A man once came to the Prophet (P.B.U.H.) and asked :
" O Messenger of Allah! Whom should I be more dutiful to ?
The Prophet (P.B.U.H.) replied: "To your mother."
The man asked: "Then to whom ?" He replied: "To your mother."
Once again the man asked: "Then to whom ?"
The prophet (P.B.U.H.) said: "To your mother."
Once again the man asked: "Then to whom?"
The Prophet (P.B.U.H.) said: "To your Father".

Ahmad/Nasaa-ee

Step 5: Pin first side of second scarf on one side of head. Bring it around and pin the furthest it can go.

Step 6: Take scarf further around head and let remaining part hang over shoulder.

• METHOD OF SWINGING •

Step 1: Swing underscarf. Use first scarf and swing around head to make smaller.

Step 2: Pin longer side of second scarf and pin on both sides of head.

Step 3: Take first colour. Bring point to front and pin where preferred. Take remaining edge bring backwards and pin.

Step 4: Pleat the inside of V, pin and tuck remaining piece away underneath underscarf.

• VARIATIONS •

1. This style can also be done with basic style II.

2. TWO-TONE LAYER EFFECT :

STEP 2 : Instead of starting on long side. Begin on shorter side.
STEP 3 : Remain the same.
STEP 4 : Take edge of second colour. Make a V and pin. Take edge of first colour . Make V and pin. Pleat inside of V and tuck away. Form as many V's as possible but keep enough scarf left to bring around neck.

• PETALS •

"Beware of the green manure."
Asked what green manure meant, he replied
"A beautiful person growing up in a bad environment."

Dar-Qutni

Use any flimsy scarf like chiffon, silk or voile with contrasting embroidery or beading. The long Dubatta scarves (Punjabi scarves) either plain or colourful can be used.

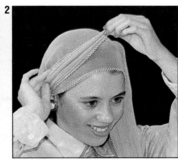

• METHOD OF SWINGING •

Step 1: Swing underscarf. If large scarf is used fold in half and place decorative edges in front. Centre long side of scarf and pin on both sides of head.

Step 2: Use first side of scarf. Form as for V but close ends (thus forming petals). Form petals, vary sizes. Tuck remaining parts away underneath underscarf.

Step 3: Use second side. pin and bring around neck. Pin on other side of head.

Step 4: Bring scarf further over head, covering the ends of petals. Either forming another petal or bringing over crown to hang on side.

• VARIATIONS •

If large wide scarf is use, fold in half and centre decorative edge of longer side of rectangle in front.

For more formal functions: Scarf can be further enhanced by forming a flower on the side of head.

Step 2: Instead of tucking remaining parts of scarf away, leave it to flow over shoulders

Step 3: The same but before starting with Step 4, bring remaining parts over scarf (It must hang over top drape).

Step 4: Follow through.

Step 5: Take remaining part of Step 2 and pin in the form of a flower.

• SLANTING PLEATS •

The Messenger of Allah (P.B.U.H.) said:

*"Whoever wants to follow my Tradition,
then marriage is my tradition."*

Muslim and Bukhari

It is narrated, too:

*"Whoever marries, safe-
guards half of his religion.
Let him take care of his duty
to the other half."*

Baihaqi

32

• SLANTING PLEATS •

Use any rectangular scarf with or without decorative edges.
Fabric should not be too flimsy. Fabric should be soft and flowing.
Pleats will be more visible with lined scarves.

• METHOD OF SWINGING •

Step 1: Swing underscarf. Centre long side of scarf. Pin on both sides of head.

Step 2: Lift first side up as far as possible above ear. Keep scarf in slanting position and pin remaining parts away.

Step 3: Make even pleats. Bring it down and around to ear on the other side of head. Pin and tuck remaining parts away.

Step 4: Use second side. Pin and bring around neck to other side and pin.

Step 5: Bring over head and pin on the other side.

• VARIATIONS •

FOR TWO TONE EFFECT:

1. Use The Two-Tone V style instead of forming a V , follow STEP 2 and STEP 3 (Slanting Pleats) and proceed with STEP 5 and STEP 6 of The V style.

2. The two-tone effect will be more effective if floral and plain scarves are used.

• DOUBLE DRAPE •

"Marry a pious person,
otherwise your hands may be filled with dust
i.e. you will enter into poverty spiritually or even materially."

Muslim/Bukhari

Use a rectangular scarf with or without beaded edge.
If preferred cords and string of pearls can be used
to further enhance this style.

• METHOD OF SWINGING •

Step 1: Make a fold of approximately 6cm on the long side of the scarf.

Step 2: Swing underscarf and pin long folded scarf about 30cm away from edge on both sides.

Step 3: Bring edge of folded part down and form halfmoon around forehead and pin.

Step 4: Use narrow side of rectangular scarf and form another halfmoon around forehead, spacing evenly.

Step 5: Use second side. Pin and bring around neck.

Step.6: Take scarf further to hang on other side.

• VARIATIONS •

1. Incorporating string of pearls:
Before starting Step.5, place cord or string of pearls between the halfmoons and tie at the back.
Proceed with STEP 5 and STEP 6.

2. Making triple layers:
Step 6: Take narrow edge of second side and form anothe halfmoon.
Step 7: Adjust and pin the back part of scarf.

3. To make Point. Follow Step 1, 2 and 3.
Step 4: Use point of one side and place in front.
Follow Step 5 and step 6 as above

• HALFMOON ROLL •

"And of His signs is this: He created mates for you from yourselves that you may find rest in them, and He ordained between you love and mercy. Most surely there are signs in this for a people who reflect."

Sura Al-Rum (30:21)

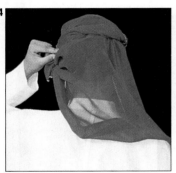

• HALFMOON ROLL •

Use a rectangular scarf with a beaded or corded edge.

• METHOD OF SWINGING •

Step 1: Swing underscarf. Centre long side of scarf and pin on both sides of head.

Step 2: Lift one side . Pin behind ears and roll (swinging to front). Spread decorated edge evenly while rolling. Stop in middle and pin.

Step 3: Skip roll letting edge form half-moon pattern on forehead. Pin.

Step 4: Roll further until the end . Pin or tie around the roll at the back of head.

Step 5: Use second side. Pin on side and take scarf further around neck.

Step 6: Pin on other side and bring over head and pin on side.

• VARIATIONS •

Finish off with

1. Band around top of roll.
2. Brooch in centre of half-moon.
3. Centre point of second side on crown of head.

IF SCARF IS TOO SHORT ; FOLLOW STYLE OF THE ROLL.

• TWO TONE TWIST ROLL •

"...Marry such a person as seems good to you."

Sura Al-Nisa (4:3)

"He it is Who created you from a single being, and of the same (kind) did He make his mate that he might incline to like her."

Sura Al-A'raf (7:189)

Use two contrasting colours. If a second rectangular scarf is used fold it to form band. Otherwise a strip of material or string of pearls will also suffice.

• METHOD OF SWINGING •

Step 1: Swing underscarf. Use second colour . Fold in band and tie at back around head. Leave to hang.

Step 2: Use main colour . Centre it and pin on both sides.

Step 3: Take band bring around to front pin and make a roll using two colours, turning one around the other.

Step 4: When reaching near middle. Pin down. Skip rolling. Pin down Start rolling and twisting until finish. Tie onto beginning of roll or tuck away underneath.

Step 5: Use remaining side. Pin up and bring around neck. Pin on other side.

Step 6: Bring over head and pin on side.

• VARIATIONS •

1. If second colour is visible (brighter colour)

STEP 1 : First tie the second colour around head and then swing underscarf over it.

2. USING PEARLS AND CORD :

STEP 3 : Slot in pearls or cord from side.

3. IF SCARF IS TOO SHORT :

STEP 1 : Start from narrow side and follow Pillbox style.

4. FOR MORE FORMAL FUNCTIONS:

Round off with brooch in centre.

5. If preferred , roll and twist all round head evenly.

• SINGLE OPENED ROLL •

It is reported by Abdullah Ibn Amr that the Prophet (P.B.U.H.) said:

*"Verily the best of you is the best to his women,
and I am the best of you to my women."*

Ibn Majar

Use any rectangular scarf.
Thicker, non-slip fabric gives a more beautiful roll.

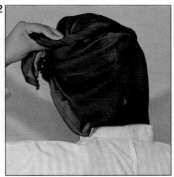

• METHOD OF SWINGING •

Step 1 : Swing underscarf. Centre long side of scarf. Pin on both sides of head.

Step 2 : Take first side, bring it up above ear. Pin on side of head. Roll side loosely and place roll   around head. Tie or pin and tuck remaining parts underneath at back.

Step 3: Gradually pull the roll open in centre of forehead.

Step 4: Use remaining side. Pin and bring around neck. Pin and bring around crown of head and pin on other side.

• VARIATIONS •

1. IF SCARF IS TOO SHORT:
Step 2: Use roll style starting at narrow side.(6.3 of Twisting Roll).

2. Pin brooch in opening.

3. TO COVER MOUTH :
Instead of swinging around neck, bring around mouth.

• TWO TONE KNOT •

"The best gift a parent can offer a child is good conduct."

Ahmad.

Use two contrasting rectangular scarves.
A rectangular scarf and a band or
strip of material of dress can be used.
Colours chosen depend on the prominent colours in outfit.

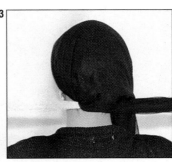

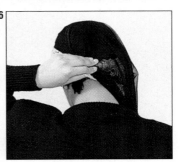

• METHOD OF SWINGING •

Step 1 : Swing underscarf. Use second colour. Fold in width of band. Tie one end around head. Leave remaining part hanging.

Step 2 : Centre long side of top (main) scarf and pin on both sides of head.

Step 3 : Take one side of top scarf and remaining part of Step 1 to back and twist it.

Step 4 : Take the two ends of Step 3 and bring it under main colour to front. Let it overlap in centre of head.

Step 5: Make a knot by bringing left side around right swopping sides in hands.

Step 6: Take both sides to the back. Tie together in knot and tuck excess away.

Step 7: Take remaining side and pin. Bring around neck.

Step 8: Take point and tuck or pin it under knot. Take sides and pin on both sides of head.

• VARIATIONS •

A Multitude of knots can be made depending on the length of the scarf.

Repeat STEPS 4, 5 and 6.

Remember : Keep the same colour on one side.

• THREE-TONE KNOT •

"...And they (women) have rights similar to those (of men) over them just in manner..."

Sura Al-Baqara (2:228)

"...live with them on a footing of kindness and equity. If you dislike it, it may be that you dislike a thing and Allah brings through it a great deal of good."

Sura Al-Nisa (4:19)

"When you have divorced women, and they have reached their prescribed term, then either retain them in honour or release them in kindness..."

Sura Al-Baqara (2:231)

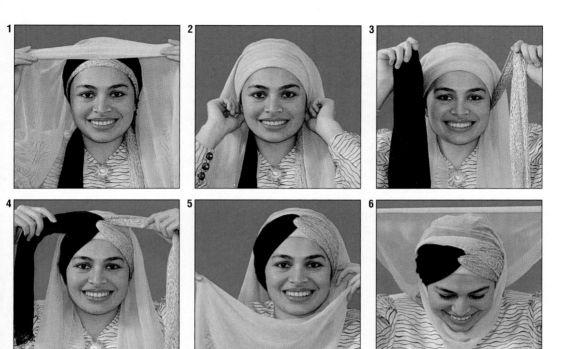

Use three contrasting rectangular scarves.
A floral scarf with two contrasting colour scarves
can be used to enhance colouring
of main floral scarf.

• METHOD OF SWINGING •

Step 1: Swing underscarf. Take the two colours chosen for making knot. Fold it the width of band, approximately 12cm wide. Tie or pin points separately around head.

Step.2: Leave the two legs of band hanging at back. Centre main scarf and pin it on both sides of head.

Step 3 : Bring the two contrasting legs to side of head. Bring to the front and make knot (as in Two- tone Knot). Repeat Steps 3 and 4 and tuck remaining parts away.

Step 4 : Take to back. Entwine and bring again to form another knot. Take to back, entwine and tuck away.

Step 5: Take one side of main scarf. Pin and bring around neck. Pin on side and take to the furthest point around head.

Step 6 : Centre and pin the point on the second side of main scarf. Adjust and pin the sides. Ruche at nape of head.

1&2

1. If bands are used to make knot, tuck ends of band underneath underscarf.
2. Follow Step 1 if two scarves are used. (This is to make the legs shorter.)
3. To make entwining colour :
Step 3 : Instead of making knot – overlap in centre of head. Take around to back , entwine and repeat.

3

4

5

4. A roll can also be formed from this style : Step 3 : Twist contrasting legs to form roll and bring around head or forehead. Double or single.

5. To form layers :
Step 3 : Instead of knot. Bring sides separately around head. Spacing layers evenly.

• LADIES IN VEIL •

A niqaab or purdah is the cloth used to cover the face.
A long dupatta scarf(see bodywraps) is swing around to cover the head
and bosoms. Most of the styles in this book can be used to cover mouths
by simply bringing edge around nose instead of only covering neck.

THE NIQAAB CAN BE

1. A rectangular piece of material, not see through about 60cm wide with an opening for the eyes. On the top edge of niqaab two pieces of self adhesive strip can be sewn to tie around head.

2. A beaded mouth piece which can be tied around face to cover the mouth.

3. A burqah - that is a semi-circular flair which sides are sewn together leaving a place for the face to come out.A niqaab with an opening made of lace is sewn onto the top of burqah.

CODE OF MODESTY IS LAID DOWN IN THE QURAN (24:31) AS FOLLOWS:

" And say to the believing women that they should lower their gaze and guard their modesty; and that they should not display their beauty and ornaments except what (must ordinarily) appear thereof.

That they should draw their veils over their bosoms and not display their beauty save to their husbands, or their fathers or their husbands' fathers, or their sons or their husbands'sons, or their brothers or their brothers' sons, or their sisters' sons or their women, or slaves whom their right hands possess, or male servants free of physical desire, or small children who have sense of sex; "

• OPEN FAN •

THE PROPHET (Peace be upon him) said :

" *A time will come upon my people when they will love five things and forget five things.*

They will love the creation and forget the Creator ,

They will love money (material things) and they will forget the reckoning ,

They will love their mansions and they will forget their graves,

They will love this world and they will forget the hereafter ,

They will love sin and they will forget about repentance. "

Kanzul-Ummaal

For those exotic women going to exotic occasions. Use a rectangular scarf, preferably a stiff fabric eg. heavier chiffon or muslin with decorative borders, either laced or scalloped edges on narrow side of scarf.

• METHOD OF SWINGING •

Step 1: Swing underscarf. Use long side of scarf. Before pinning, measure length needed to make fan.

Step 2: Pin on both sides of head. Bring shorter side round the back, underneath the longer side and keep on side.

Step 3: Take the chosen edge. Fold or pleat and bring to side or back of head.

Step 4: Position fan (back or side). Pin fan firmly to remain in position.

Step 5: Take remaining side. Bring to front and pin on side.

Step 6: Bring side around neck and pin on other side.

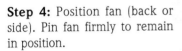

• VARIATIONS •

1. Fan can either be placed at back or on the side of head.

2. A fan at back can also be formed by :Step 3 : take shorter side to back and place fan at the back of head. Keep folds together and pin in position.

3. An easier way is to tie elastic band around the part of the scarf you want to use as the fan.

Size of the fan depends on the width of the decorative edge or own choice.

• THE FLOWER •

The Prophet (P.B.U.H.) said:

"A woman whose husband is pleased with her at the time of her death goes straight to paradise."

This style is more or less the same as the Fan style but it does not stand upright and it also has some ruching . It is suitable to wear to more formal functions. Use preferably a more flimsy rectangular scarf with beaded embroidered or scalloped edge.

• METHOD OF SWINGING •

Step 1 : Swing underscarf. Start from long side of scarf. Take one side, make allowance for part to hang and part to form flower.

Step 2 : Tie elastic band or cotton around parts for hanging and flower. Follow as in STEP 2 of Open Fan style.

Step 3: Fold or pleat side. Place at middle of head. Leave part of scarf and decorative edge to hang loose.

Step 4: Arrange border to form pattern and secure by pinning. Ruche and form flower by pinning.

Step 5: Pin remaining side on one side of head and bring around to cover neck. Pin on other side.

Step 6: Take further around head underneath flower and pin.

• VARIATION 1 •

TO EMPHASISE THE FLOWER MORE

Step 1: Instead of starting with long bordered edge, place plain side in front.

Step 5: Instead of bringing the bordered side around neck, bring plain side around neck.

• VARIATION 2 •

TWO-TONE FLOWER

*If second colour is a long scarf, follow Step 1
of Two -tone style.*
If shorter band is used do as follows:

Step 2: Pin on both sides of head. Take edge of second colour and slot in underneath. Take second colour underneath shorter side and bring around back, underneath longer side. Keep on side.

Step 3: Remain the same but when bringing around head, two colours will hang loose. Keep second colour under first or next to it.

Step 4: Remain the same, but arrange so that two-tone is formed.

Step 5: Take edges of border one longer than the other and follow step through.

Step 6: Remain the same.

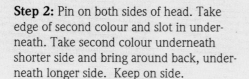

*"And give women their dowries as a free gift, but if they themselves be
pleased to give up to you a portion of it, then eat it with enjoyment and
with wholesome result."*

Holy Quran 4:4

• LOOSE BANDS •

Tirmithi Ibn Majah and Mushad Ahmad narrates that:

"The one who wears the clothes for name and fame in this world, Allah will clothe that person with clothes of disgrace on the day of Judgement and will light the fire of Hell in those clothes."

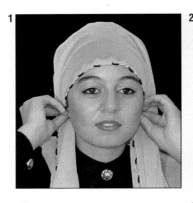

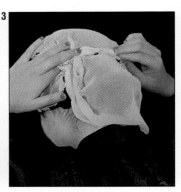

This style is quite common amongst the Muslim community in Johannesburg and Durban. For this style you can either use a triangular scarf with or without decorative edges. This style can also be swung without underscarf, depending on type of fabric used.

• METHOD OF SWINGING •

Step 1: Swing underscarf. Centre scarf and pin at both sides of the head 'temporarily'.

Step 2: Pin one side as high as possible above and behind ear-lobe.

Step 3: Roll side (by turning edge around). Place roll around head as far as possible. Pin or tie onto start.

Step 4: Take out pins and pull front carefully out under roll. Make a wavy pattern on forehead.

Step 5: Bring other side around neck. Do not pull too hard and pin at back and sides of head.

• VARIATIONS •

This effect you will also get by incorporating bands to the basic rectangular style.
Use the rope or material bands.

Step 5: The same but cover back of band with scarf.

• VARIATION WITH BANDS •

Fancy caps, scarves and various bands (plaited, sequined, beaded, etc.)
can be used. These bands can be worn for various occasions.
The more elegant or elaborate ones for formal occasions
and plainer ones for more informal occasions.
These bands can be incorporated with either Basic Style I or II.
I find it much better using Basic Style II.

• METHOD OF SWINGING •

Step 1 : Swing underscarf. Centre long side of scarf and pin both sides of head.

Step 2 : Incorporate various bands. See ideas for bands below. Adjust band on or around head and secure by pinning.

Step 3 & 4 follow Basic style II

• VARIATIONS •

1. TWO - TONE KNOT	2. BORDERED ROLL	3. FOLDED BORDERS
Take two contrasting rectangular bands or scarves folded in form of a band. Take both scarves (keeping it next to each other), place around back and make knot in front as in Two-Tone style.	Take bordered edge of scarf. Keep bulk of scarf steady while swinging only border around bulk of scarf. Place around head and pin at back. Tuck excess away.	Fold scarf bringing out desired pattern. Place around front of head and tie at the back. This can also be incorporated after completing STEP 4, let a part hang loose at back.

4. TWO-TONE PLAITED BAND

Use six strips of colourful narrow bands (3 strips per colour) Nylon stocking can also be used. Plait to get effect in picture.

5. FANCY CAPS

Look at underscarf-caps for ideas. To prevent moving, put cap on head and pin onto scarf. (Secure cap neatly). Pin last side bringing out decorative edge.

6. MATERIAL BANDS

Use two or three strips or bands matching fabric of outfit. Sew the edges on one side. Twist or plait and sew together on the other side. Sew elastic on sides to place around head.

7. PILLBOX

Cut out desired pattern on soft cardboard. Use fabric matching outfit. Cover pattern. Pleats can also be formed. (See picture). Sew elastic on edge or cut it long enough to fit around head.

"Apart from cases of ill-treatment and genuine aversion of wife against husband, Islam recognises other grounds of divorce also.

These are:

1. *option of puberty.*
2. *refusal to provide economic sustenance.*
3. *change of religion.*
4. *impotence.*
5. *infectious diseases in either partner.*
6. *wilfull desertion.*
7. *disappearance of partner."*

Women in Islam by M.M.Siddiqi

BASIC TRIANGULAR
— SCARF —

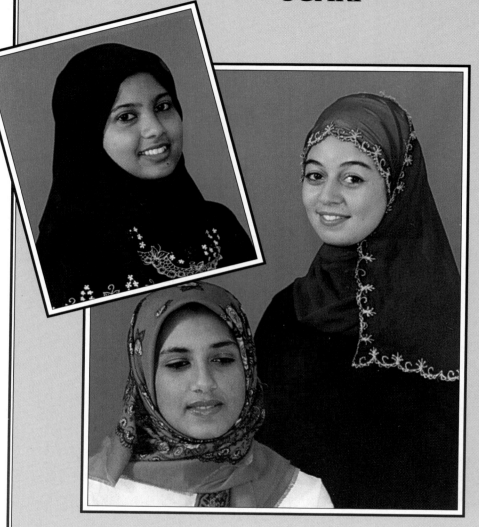

"Man is the ruler in his home. He will be held responsible
for the conduct of his dependants
and women is the ruler in her husband's home.
She will also be held responsible for the conduct of her dependants."

Bukhari

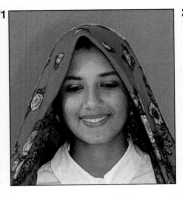

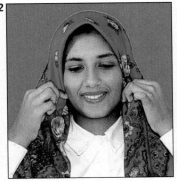

This style can be swung using any rectangular, triangular and square scarf.

• METHOD OF SWINGING •

Step 1: If scarf is slippery, swing underscarf, otherwise not. If a square scarf is used, fold diagonally to form a triangular shape and centre on head.

Step 2: With index finger and thumb, hold front edges of scarf. Press edge of scarf just under cheekbone with index finger down in circular movement, swinging thumbs and scarf to front and edge to the back.

Step 3: Keep scarf in that position. Move finger further down underneath ear, pulling edge tighter.

Step 4: Under chin, keep rolled edge in left hand steady while bringing right hand around neck.

Step 5: Take further (Bring right) around head and tuck away on side. Let left hand side go.

• VARIATIONS •

Step 5: Instead of tucking away,
Use a brooch on chain or string of small flowers etc.
to pin on side where right scarf was brought over.

• HINT •

The technique lies in the holding down of the one side while the other side is swung around.

BASIC ROLL STYLE WITH
— TRIANGULAR SCARF —

"O children of Adam! Wear your beautiful apparel at everytime and place of prayer; eat and drink; but waste not by excess, for Allah loveth not the wasters."

Quran 7:31

1

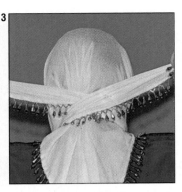

2

3

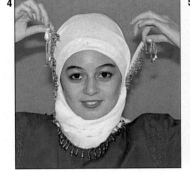

4

5

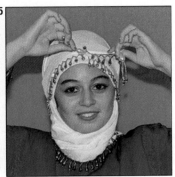

• IDEAS •

Use a large square or triangular scarf with or without decorative edges. The sides must be long enough to go around head.

• METHOD OF SWINGING •

Step 1: With or without underscarf. Fold scarf in triangular shape and centre it.

Step 2: Follow Step 2 and Step 3 of Basic Triangular style.

Step 3: Take both sides. Bring around under chin. Swop in opposite hands and take to back.

Step 4: At back swing around one another and fold or roll sides highlighting decorative edges and bring to front.

Step 5: Make knot as in Two - tone Knot style. Take edges to back as far as possible and tuck away under fold.

• VARIATIONS •

1. Place roll in front and pull bottom a little to front to make wavy patterns on forehead.

2. Do not roll, fold and place around front to form a 'V'.

3. Do not make a knot just overlap in front and pin a brooch .

• TWO TONE TRIANGULAR ROLL •

It is reported that Ibn Abbas (R.A.) said:

"I used to beautify myself for my wife exactly in the manner she beautified herself for me and I have based this behaviour on the verse in the Qur'an: 'They have rights similar to those (of men) over them in a just manner'."

Tafsir : Maraghi

Use two square scarves, a triangular scarf with contrasting band or a triangular scarf with contrasting borders.

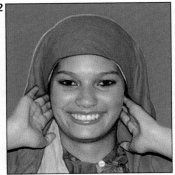

• METHOD OF SWINGING •

Step 1: If using two square scarves, fold one colour the width of a band. Place the band around head and tie or pin at the back.

Step 2: Centre second triangular scarf on head and pin both sides of head using the band as the underscarf.

Step 3: Bring one leg of scarf and band above earlobe and pin.

Step 4: Twist colour evenly around forehead. Pin roll on the other side or tie onto beginning of roll.

Step 5: Bring second leg of scarf around to cover neck.

• VARIATIONS •

Roll can be placed around forehead or to the back of head.

• THE TRIANGULAR V •

"Your Lord has decreed that you worship none save Him,
and (you show) kindness to your parents.
If one of them or both of them reach old age with you,
say not 'Fie' to them nor repulse them,
but speak to them a generous word.
And make yourself submissively gentle with compassion
and say: Oh Lord! Have mercy on them both
as they did care for me (when I was) little."

Sura Bani Israel (17:23 & 24)

Use a triangular scarf or fold a square scarf in triangular shape. Scarves must have beautiful embroidered or beaded edges. For a more elegant feature, borders could be contrasting.

• METHOD OF SWINGING •

Step 1: With or without underscarf. Centre scarf on head and pin on both sides of head.

Step 2: Pin decorative edge of first side of scarf below ear. Let decorative edge point downwards.

Step 3: Take edge, bring to centre of head or where preferred and pin.

Step 4: Take remaining edge back to the side of head, pin or tuck away (thus forming a V).

Step 5: Pleat the inside of the V and pin down the sides.

Step 6: Pin second side around neck and let remaining part hang loose.

• VARIATIONS •

1. The V's can be formed at any angle preferred.
2. A multitude of V's can be formed depending on size of the triangle used.
3. See Petal style for more ideas.
4. For more formal functions make bow or pin flowers on side.

• THE PILLBOX TRIANGULAR •

"When one of you wants to marry a woman,
he says (to the guardian)
'I accept the covenant taken by Allah' : . And then
(a woman) must be retained in honour or released in kindness."

Urf

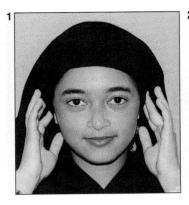

Use a triangular scarf or a square scarf and fold in a triangle. Scarves must have decorative edge either embroidered, beaded or fringed. Contrasting borders give a better effect.

• METHOD OF SWINGING •

Step 1: With or without underscarf. Centre scarf and pin both sides of head.

Step 2: Bring first side of scarf high up and secure by pinning.

Step 3: Bring folded edge around forehead. Pin in middle.

Step 4: Take remaining edge and bring further around head if possible to the beginning. Pin or tie at back of head.

Step 5: Take second side and pin on side and bring around neck. Pin on other side and bring edge further around.

• VARIATIONS •

Instead of folding:
Step 2: Roll side spreading edges evenly around head.

• CHIGNON •

The Prophet (P.B.U.H.) said:

"The husband should address his wife in order to bring happiness to her."

Tirmithi

This style, designed by Aslam Pieterse, is especially for those with long hair although those with short hair can also use it. Read below. Use a flimsy rectangular scarf with or without decorative edge, although beaded edges will enhance the style even further.

• METHOD OF SWINGING •

Step 1: Make hair in a pony-tail. Swing underscarf letting the poni-tail out.

Step 2: Centre narrow side of rectangular scarf, pin or tie at back.

Step 3: Roll the scarf around hair evenly (not too thick). Keep a piece to make petals.

Step 4: Take rolled part and make a pattern with it on the side of head, pinning the roll tightly.

Step 5: Now form petals. (See petal style). Vary sizes and position of petals.

Step 6: Ruche the part between roll and petals, thus forming gathers. While pinning down.

• VARIATIONS •

1. If hair is too short:
Use a band or second colour and tuck underneath.

2. Two tone roll and two tone petals:
Use a band or scarf in contrasting colour.

Step 1: If scarf is used, swing second colour first under or on top of underscarf OR tuck band underneath.

Step 2 : Divide the pony-tail in two.

Step 3 : Roll scarves separately around hair.

Step 4 : The same as above.

Step 5 : Same but alternate colour of petals or form petals by placing contrasting colour on top of each other.

Step 6 : The same but entwine colours.

• THE PLAIT •

Allah is very pleased with the women of the An-sar because shyness did not prevent them from improving their knowledge about Islam.

Bukhari

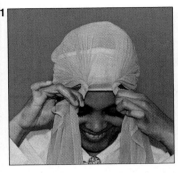

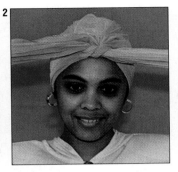

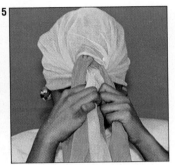

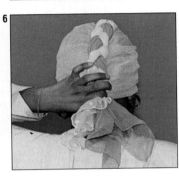

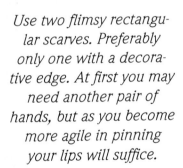

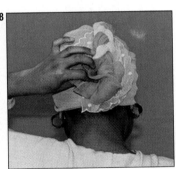

Use two flimsy rectangular scarves. Preferably only one with a decorative edge. At first you may need another pair of hands, but as you become more agile in pinning your lips will suffice.

• METHOD OF SWINGING •

Step 1: Swing underscarf. Centre long side of second scarf around back of head. Bring sides to front.

Step 2: Take the two sides of scarf roll it to the inside and make knot in front.

Step 3: Take main colour. Pin at back (temporarily to prevent slipping). Roll and make knot in front behind first knot.

Step 4: Roll three sides (preferably two of top and one side of bottom scarf) not too tight and keep in mouth or let someone hold. Roll the remaining side in front and pin in any design of choice.

Step 5: Bring rolls to back and start plaiting. Until just enough to reach back edge of scarf.

Step 6: Pin plait at the edge of scarf and secure.

Step 7: Tuck the two points underneath plait to form a leaf.

Step 8: Form flower or any pattern with two of remaining rolls.

• VARIATIONS •

TWO-TONE FISH PLAIT :

Steps 1, 2 & 3 remain the same.
Step 4: Roll one side of top colour a third of the way.
Bring it around other sides and pin (let it form two circles).
The remaining part use as the fourth leg for the fish plait.
Step 5: Do fish plait as follows :
Steps 6, 7 and 8 remain the same.

The Prophet (P.B.U.H.) said:

"Have a look at her\him that is before marriage in order to bring about a lasting love and affection between the two of you."

Ibn Majah / Ibn Hibban

• TURBAN STYLING •

*Using a rectangular, a square folded into a triangule
or a triangular scarf with or without decorative edges.
To incorporate with dress use same fabric as dress.
The stiffer fabric forms a more visible roll.
Bands, strings of pearls, etc. can be used to form variation.*

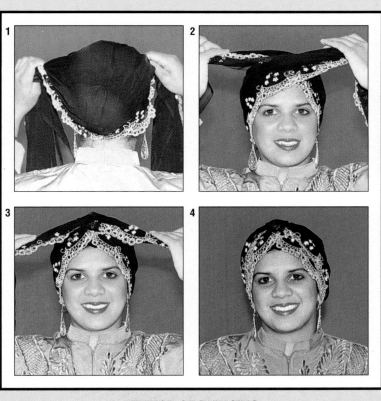

• METHOD OF SWINGING •

Step 1: Centre scarf around the back of head.

Step 2: Hold two sides at front on both sides of head with point hanging over forehead.

Step 3: Overlap both legs of scarves in centre of head. Take opposite legs further to back.

Step 4: Open point or fold it smaller and tuck underneath or pin point to the back.

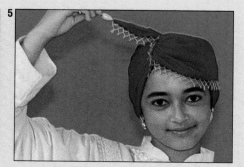

1. Triangular scarves.

Follow instructions Step 1 and 2.

Step.3. Instead of overlapping both sides, twist in middle. Then take away one leg further and tuck it away.

Step 4: Keep the second leg hanging loose and complete as in Step.4. above.

Step 5: Bring second leg over centre to form drape on forehead.

---

2. Use preferred rectangular or triangular scarves.

Follow instructions Step 1 and 2.

Step 3: Bring legs in front. Twist legs to make a thick roll.

Step 4: Place roll vertically down the middle and tuck excess away.

• TWO TONE TURBANS •

ENTWINING COLOUR

TWO TONE KNOT

TWO TONE LAYERS

ENTWINING ROLL

Various styles can be created using two contrasting rectangular scarves or a rectangular scarf and a strip of fabric matching the outfit.

• METHOD OF SWINGING •

ENTWINING COLOUR

Step 1: If using two rectangular scarves, swing underscarf. Centre and tie narrow side of both scarves separately around head.

Step 2: Take the legs of the two scarves. Twist it at the back and bring it to the side of head. Use first leg, fold and swing around head and bring again to the starting position.

Step 3: Do the same to the second leg, but when reaching the other side, fold slightly narrower. Repeat steps 2 and 3 depending on length of scarf. Try to swing folded side everytime further away.

Step 4: Tie remaining edge and make rose bud on side using excess scarf.
OR
Step 4: Tuck one leg underneath. Pin the edge of second leg to hang loose on side.

Edge of second leg hanging loose.

"They, the women, are a garment unto you and you are a garment unto them."

Surah 2 : 187

And if you wish to have (one) wife in the place of another and you have given one of them a heap of gold (as dowry) take not anything from her, would you take by slandering (her) and (doing her) manifest wrong?"

Quran 4:20

ENTWINING ROLL OR LAYERS

Centre and pin narrow side on both sides of head.

Step 2: Take both legs to the same side.

Step 3: Start layering twisting to form one or two rolls around head.

TWO-TONE KNOT.

Step 1 and 2 remain the same.

Step 3: Form knot or knots as in two-tone knot style.

Another easy way to create a Two-Tone Turban effect is by swinging a scarf as in underscarf styling. Take second scarf, band or strip of material and tie around first scarf to form knot in front, a bow in front or on side, or even a flower.

BACK VIEW FOR TURBAN STYLING.

Here are a few ideas what to do with excess scarves at the back of head. Instead of tucking away try the following:

Midora

The Midora, that is a square chiffon scarf approximately 114cm wide decorated with either gold or silver embroidered flowers or lines, signifies purity. In South Africa, Midoras are traditionally worn and used on occasions such as :

1. Pilgrims (Hujjaaj or Haji's) returning home from their pilgrimage to Mecca.

2. When celebrating Moulidun Nabi, a feast that marks the Prophet Muhammad PBUH 's birthday.

3. By the bride on her wedding day. It is customary that virtuous brides wear a midora on their wedding day as a sign of purity as in virginity.

4. Worn by Haji's (people who performed their pilgrimage to Mecca). Traditionally a few Haji's are sent by the bridegroom to fetch his wife and to bring her to his chambers. This proceeding usually ends the wedding ceremony.

5. At the Christening, that is the naming of a newborn baby which traditionally takes place the seventh day after birth. On this occasion the baby is placed on a pillow, wrapped in a midora and decorated with flowers such as carnations, rosebuds etc.

HINTS FOR PINNING MIDORA FOR HAJIS

Styling a Midora for occasions 1, 2, and 4 that will be worn by Haji's is easy. All you really need is to be creative.

1. Midoras can be pinned on an undercap or "a mould" can be used to give more height and form to the style (See bridal styling). These undercaps should be adjustable so that the Midora can be removed from the head and still remain intact.

2. Long, thin stainless steel pins are necessary in order not to make holes in the fabric.

3. For Haji's it is important to have the neck covered. Thus always establish first how to cover the neckline. Keeping it in mind, you can start styling the Midora.

STARTING POSITIONS:

3.1 The starting position is to centre the edge of the Midora on head. (As in highlighting Petals)
3.2 Pin edge of Midora more to end on both sides of head.
(See Layering and Slanting Petals)

4. After pinning Midora on head and establishing what side will be used to cover neck and neckline. The remaining two sides can now be used to create different design, be it folds, petals, flowers, etc.

The Holy Qur'an says : (2:143)

"Thus have We made of you an Ummat
Justly balanced (of the middle path).
That ye might be witnesses
over the nations ..."

• HIGHLIGHTING THE FLOWER •

Rules of dress when a woman reaches old age.

THE QURAN SAYS (24:60)

"Such elderly women as are past the prospect of marriage, there is no blame on them if they lay aside their (outer) garments, provided they make not a wanton display of their beauty; ...but it is best for them to be modest and Allah is the One who sees and knows all things. "

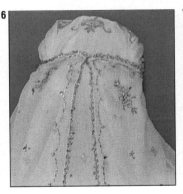

Use a Midora with flower in centre of one of the edges of the square.

• METHOD OF SWINGING •

STEP 1 : Centre opposite edge of flower designed edge (on wrong side of Midora) and pin on both sides of head.

STEP 2 : Bring the flower design over head and centre on forehead. Take side of flower to the back forming a halfmoon.

STEP 3 : Bring the remaining edge of STEP 2 down and place on side of head to form a petal (See petals). Do the same to the other side.

STEP 4 : Take the remaining corner and bring it centre back. Pin both points at back of head.

STEP 5 : Use remaining edges of STEP 1 and cover neck.

STEP 6 : The back can be worn as above OR

STEP 7 : Rosebud can now be formed by bringing edges around the gold motiff. (See picture)

• SLANTING PETALS •

*"Beware of a building called the 'Public Bath'.
Some people said, 'O Messenger of Allah, it certainly
removes dirt and benefits the sick.' He then said,
'Then whoever enters should cover his nakedness'"*

Al-Hakim

• SLANTING PETALS •

*For this style do not use a mould that is
too high rather use a stiff fez and cover it with an
underscarf. Petal forming will be done from
the right hand side clockwise using
the edge of midora.*

• METHOD OF SWINGING •

Step 1 : Start near edge of one side and pin on both sides of head. Longer side should be kept for covering neck.

Step 2 : Take first edge of one side and make slanting petals in front.

Step 3 : Take third edge and form 3 petals pointing to crown at the back.

Step 4 : Take narrow side of front edge (right hand side) and form a V to half slanting petals.

Step 5 : Take long side of front edge (left hand side). Pin to form petal.

Step 6 : Take excess. Cover neck and pin on right hand side.

"Lodge them where you dwell, according to your means, and harass them not as to straiten life for them. And if they are pregnant, then spend for them till they bring forth their burden. Then, if they give suckle for you, give them their due payment and enjoin one another among you to do good; but if you disagree, then let other (woman) suckle for him (the father of the child). Let him who has abundance spend of his abundance, and he whose provision is measured, let him spend of that which Allah has given him; Allah does not lay a burden on any soul, except that which He has given it. Allah will bring about ease after hardship."

Sura Al-Talaq
(65:6,7)

• LAYERING BORDER •

Use a broader mould to give height. Start from the left hand side and work anti-clockwise around the edge to form layers.

• METHOD OF SWINGING •

Step 1 : Centre midora and pin on both sides of head.

Step 2 : Bring first edge round to form double layers by using index finger and pin on both sides of head.

Step 3 : Make as many layers as possible spacing edges evenly from side to side.

Step 4 : When forming last layer instead of bringing it back to side form a 'V' at back of head.

Step 5 : Bring first side around to cover neck.

Step 6 : Bring other side round to cover neck.

• PILLBOX MIDORA •

"The Prophet's (P.B.U.H.) educational circles in the masjid was attended by many females".

"For Eid Prayers almost all women participated in the gathering and the Prophet (P.B.U.H.) used to move to the place where they were seated at the back and spoke to them."

Al-Hadith Wal Muhaddithu by Muhammad Abuzahw.

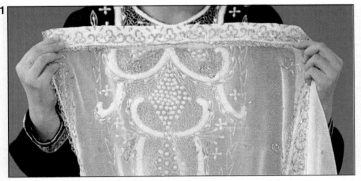

1

2

3

4

5

6

7

Use a midora with border, a strip of soft cardboard to form band and handkerchief.

• METHOD OF SWINGING •

STEP 1: Cut strip of cardboard and cover it with handkerchief(BAND).Cover band with midora bringing out desired border.Tuck or pin to keep intact.

STEP 2: Adjust undercap and pin midora near point on both sides of head. The band will hang point down on the side.

STEP 3: Adjust band around head and secure by pinning.

STEP 4: Cover neck with excess part of step 3.

STEP 5: Make a flower with excess of Step 4.

STEP 6: Adjust folds around neck .Pinning the other side.

STEP 7: Use the back part to form flowers or pattern at back.

QURAN (Q.XLII:23)

*"And if anyone earns any good,
We shall give him an increase
in beauty (and good) in respect thereof."*

87

The Messenger of Allah (PBUH) has said:
"The best women of my people are the
most beautiful, but who ask the lowest
possible 'mehr' (marriage portion)."

Abu Dawood

• MIDORAS – BRIDAL •

The styling of Midora is very intricate. Depending on few basic rules and a sense of creativity, you will be able to pin it.
As there are multitudes of bridal styling and because there are so many steps involved, I will try just to give you the basis for pinning a Midora and leave the rest for you to experiment.

WHAT YOU NEED

1. Thin hat wire.
2. Long thin pins.
3. A needle and cotton to sew on wire.
4. Midora (colour of your choice).
5. Mould - made of buckrim or soft cardboard.
6. Fabric or handkerchief to cover mould.
7. Tihara, flower, beads, etc. to further enhance styling.
8. Veiling to hang down the back.

PREPARE THE FOLLOWING BEFORE COMMENCING PINNING.

1. Mould :

This is like a skull cap made of either bakrim or cardboard. It gives the form when pinning. I find making it from a soft cardboard to be the cheapest. After mould is cut out, it is covered with fabric (depending on colour) to enable pinning. See diagram below for preparing instructions :

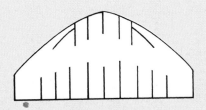 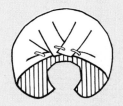 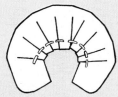

2. Preparing the Midora

As Midoras are made of chiffon, hat wire is used to form various designs. A good Midora pinner will respect your Midora and try not to spoil it. When threading the Midora it is best for him/her to tack the wire onto the edge of Midora. The number of sides that is being threaded depends on the style involved.

Another way of threading a scarf is by pushing the thin hat wire through the hem of the Midora. This way spoils the Midora.

2.1 Thread the Midora as follows :

Do not thread all sides as parts must be used to pin onto mould.

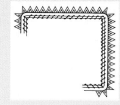

3. Forming Petals

It is best to form petals the desired size and turn cotton around it before starting to pin onto head.

Thus after the sides were threaded form petals

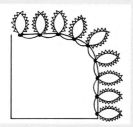

PETAL

4. METHODS OF SWINGING

1. Adjust mould on head tying end of fabric at back of head.

2. Form petals in desired style eg.

3. Take sides of Midora that is not threaded and place around mould.

4. The excess of the Midora can now be used to make patterns on the back, side or in front.

5. Sometimes most of the Midoras are used for styling then it is best to use a chiffon scarf matching the Midora.

6. Tihara and flowers can be incorporated if desired.

7. Veiling can be pinned to hang down the back.

5. CARING OF MIDORA

Midoras are nowadays very expensive and some families possess only one which is at times not the colour needed for a specific occasion.

After using take pins out carefully without tearing fabric or points.

When ironing the Midora, place paper or fabric over it. Fold it by wrapping in soft fabric and store in a safe place. If your points looks dilapidated, nowadays it is taken back to the manufacturers for rethreading.

• BODY SCARVES •

Another effective way of wearing a scarf, is by draping it around the body, thus concealing the body curves due to tight fitting dresses, low cut necks etc.

These body scarves can vary in sizes depending on what it's purpose is. It can vary from handkerchief that can be swung around your neck to long scarves which can be draped over the head as well as the body.

These long rectangular scarves known as Dupattas, are approximately 2m long. The effect of draping these scarves depends on the decoration of the scarf as well as the decoration and design of the outfit..

THE FOLLOWING ARE SOME EASY DRAPES :

1. Drapings around neckline.

2. Forming a V around neckline.

3. Draping : bringing out corners of scarves.

4. Draping : bringing out front pattern.

• WOOLEN SCARVES AND CAPS •

*"And if you fear you cannot act fairly towards the orphans,
then marry such women, who seem good to you, two or three
or four; and if you fear that you cannot do justice (between them)
then (marry) only one or that your that your rights hands possess;
this is more proper that you may not deviate from the right course."*

Sura Al-Nisa (4:3)

*To brave the cold weather, designer Aziza
Abrahams, designed some stunning designs
of woollen scarves and caps.*